Black
Achievement
IN SCIENCE

Space

Black
Achievement
IN SCIENCE

Biology

Chemistry

Computer Science

Engineering

Environmental Science

Inventors

Medicine

Physics

Space

Technology

Black
Achievement
IN SCIENCE

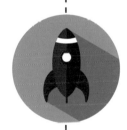

Space

By MARI RICH

Foreword by Malinda Gilmore and Mel Poulson, National Organization for the Advancement of Black Chemists and Chemical Engineers

Mason Crest
450 Parkway Drive, Suite D
Broomall, PA 19008
www.masoncrest.com

Series ISBN: 978-1-4222-3554-6
Hardback ISBN: 978-1-4222-3563-8
EBook ISBN: 978-1-4222-8330-1

First printing
1 3 5 7 9 8 6 4 2

Produced by Shoreline Publishing Group LLC
Santa Barbara, California
Editorial Director: James Buckley Jr.
Designer: Patty Kelley
Production: Sandy Gordon
www.shorelinepublishing.com
Cover photographs: Laurence Agron/Dreamstime; NASA (bkgd)

Library of Congress Cataloging-in-Publication Data

Names: Rich, Mari, author.
Title: Space / by Mari Rich ; foreword by Malinda Gilmore, Ph.D., Executive Board Chair and Mel Poulson, Executive Board Vice-Chair, National Organization for the Professional Advancement of Black Chemists and Chemical Engineers (NOBCChE).
Description: Broomall, PA : Mason Crest, [2017] | Series: Black achievement in science | Includes bibliographical references and index.
Identifiers: LCCN 2016002449 | ISBN 9781422235638 (hardback) | ISBN 9781422235546 (series) | ISBN 9781422283301 (ebook) Subjects: LCSH: African American scientists--Biography--Juvenile literature. | African American astronauts--Biography--Juvenile literature. | African American engineers--Biography--Juvenile literature. | Space sciences--Biography--Juvenile literature. | Outer space--Exploration--History--Juvenile literature.
Classification: LCC TL793 .R524 2017 | DDC 520.922--dc23
LC record available at http://lccn.loc.gov/2016002449

Contents

Key Icons to Look for

Words to Understand: These words with their easy-to-understand definitions will increase the reader's understanding of the text, while building vocabulary skills.

Research Projects: Readers are pointed toward areas of further inquiry connected to each chapter. Suggestions are provided for projects that encourage deeper research and analysis.

Text-Dependent Questions: These questions send the reader back to the text for more careful attention to the evidence presented here.

Series Glossary of Key Terms: This back-of-the-book glossary contains terminology used throughout this series. Words found here increase the reader's ability to read and comprehend higher-level books and articles in this field.

Educational Videos: Readers can view videos by scanning our QR codes, providing them with additional educational content to supplement the text. Examples include news coverage, moments in history, speeches, iconic moments, and much more!

Science, Technology, Engineering and Mathematics (STEM) are vital to our future, the future of our country, the future of our regions, and the future of our children. STEM is everywhere and it shapes our everyday experiences. Science and technology have become the leading foundation of global development. Both subjects continue to improve the quality of life as new findings, inventions, and creations emerge from the basis of science. A career in a STEM discipline is a fantastic choice and one that should be explored by many.

In today's society, STEM is becoming more diverse and even internationalized. However, the shortage of African Americans and other minorities, including women, still exists. This series—***Black Achievement in Science***—reveals the numerous career choices and pathways that great African-American scientists, technologists, engineers, and mathematicians have pursued to become successful in a STEM discipline. The purpose of this series of books is to inspire, motivate, encourage, and educate people about the numerous career choices and pathways in STEM. We applaud the authors for sharing the experiences of our forefathers and foremothers and ultimately increasing the number of people of color in STEM and, more

By Malinda Gilmore, NOBCChE Executive Board Chair and Mel Poulson, NOBCChE Executive Board Vice-Chair

specifically, increasing the number of African Americans to pursue careers in STEM.

The personal experiences and accomplishments shared within are truly inspiring and gratifying. It is our hope that by reading about the lives and careers of these great scientists, technologists, engineers, and mathematicians, the reader might become inspired and totally committed to pursue a career in a STEM discipline and say to themselves, "If they were able to do it, then I am definitely able to do it, and this, too, can be me." Hopefully, the reader will realize that these great accomplishments didn't come easily. It was because of hard work, perseverance, and determination that these chosen individuals were so successful.

As Executive Board Members of The National Organization for the Professional Advancement of Black Chemists and Chemical Engineers (NOBCChE) we are excited about this series. For more than 40 years, NOBCChE has promoted the STEM fields and its mission is to build an eminent cadre of people of color in STEM. Our mission is in line with the overall purpose of this series and we are indeed committed to inspiring our youth to explore and contribute to our country's future in science, technology, engineering, and mathematics.

We encourage all readers to enjoy the series in its entirety and identify with a personal story that resonates well with you. Learn more about that person and their career pathway, and you can be just like them.

Historians believe that humans have dreamed of space flight since ancient times, pointing to rudimentary rockets devised by the Chinese for ceremonial purposes as early as the third century. It was not until the latter half of the 20th century, however, that science and technology had advanced far enough to make human space travel a possibility. In 1958, the National Aeronautics and Space Administration (NASA) initiated Project Mercury, with the objective of launching a manned spacecraft into orbital flight around the Earth and investigating human ability to function in space. The men chosen for the task of piloting the spacecraft were to be called "astronauts," a term that was coined based on the tale of the ancient Greek Argonauts, adventurers who boldly explored the unknown.

Alan Shepard being hauled up into a rescue chopper

The first manned mission took place in 1961, when astronaut Alan B. Shepard boarded the spacecraft Freedom 7 for a suborbital flight lasting 15 minutes and 28 seconds.

Astronaut Neil Armstrong on the Moon, in a famous photograph taken by Buzz Aldrin.

Project Mercury lasted slightly over four years and included six manned missions completed. An estimated 2,000,000 workers from both government agencies and private companies used their skills, knowledge, and experience for that national effort.

Following the successful Mercury missions, the idea of manned spaceflight excited the world's imagination even further, and on July 20, 1969, when Neil Armstrong became the first person ever to walk on the Moon, an estimated 600 million people—a fifth of the entire population of the Earth at the time—watched the televised event.

Among those who dreamed of participating one day in space exploration—if not as astronauts, then as scientists, researchers, technologists, and inventors—were numerous African Americans. In the years that followed, some of those

people became vital parts of the world space science community. Some men and women of color did indeed reach outer space, while others created technologies and processes that advanced the exploration of space. The opportunities were sometimes harder to create for African Americans than for others, but the hard work was worth it, and those pioneers have opened doors for thousands since.

Addressing an audience at the John F. Kennedy Space

President Obama and his family toured a NASA facility to get an up-close look at the Space Shuttle.

Center in 2010, President Barack Obama stressed the importance of the chosen field of those space science pioneers. Space research has, he asserted, "contributed to immeasurable technological advances that have improved our health and well-being, from satellite navigation to water purification, from aerospace manufacturing to medical imaging. And leading the world to space helped America achieve new heights of prosperity here on Earth, while demonstrating the power of a free and open society to harness the ingenuity of its people."

As NASA scientists outline ambitious future goals of landing humans on Mars, providing Internet access to every corner of the globe (no matter how remote), better predicting catastrophic weather events, and a host of others, more people will be needed to do the research, invent and build essential equipment, provide technical support, and perform innumerable other tasks. Some of those people will have African ancestry about which they are just as proud as they are about goals they achieve in space science. The increase in knowledge in this and all scientific fields can only be complete when everyone has a chance to play a part and make a contribution. ●

Words to Understand

nebulae
clouds of gas and dust in outer space

planetarium
a building or room in which various celestial images and effects are projected onto the walls and ceiling

propagation
the transmission of light or sound through a substance

Chapter 1

George Carruthers

Born:
1939

Nationality.
American

Achievements:
**Engineer and inventor who
created key parts of early
Apollo missions**

When Apollo 16 was launched from the Kennedy Space Center on April 16, 1972, it carried an ultraviolet (UV) camera designed by George Carruthers. The 50-pound, gold-plated apparatus was set up on the surface of the Moon and provided an unprecedented look at Earth's atmosphere, allowing for the measurement of concentrations of pollutants and providing images of more than 500 stars, **nebulae**, and galaxies.

"One of the things that [made my work] very exciting and interesting is that in the early days of the space program almost every flight was something that was breaking new ground," he said when he was inducted into the National Inventors Hall of Fame in 2003, "especially in the astronomy area, where we were previously limited to telescopes from the ground."

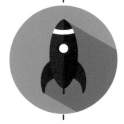

Carruthers was born on October 1, 1939, in Cincinnati, Ohio. His father, George Carruthers, Sr., was a civil engineer who served in the US Army Air Corps. His mother, Sophia, was a homemaker. From an early age, Carruthers, the oldest of four siblings, loved science. An avid builder of model rockets and reader of science fiction, he created his own telescope when he was ten, using lenses he ordered from a catalog and a cardboard tube. He paid for his catalog order with wages he had earned as a delivery boy.

When Carruthers was just twelve years old, his father died suddenly. Sophia and her children moved back to her native Chicago and she found work with the US Postal Service. Carruthers attended Chicago's Englewood High School, and became one of the few African-American students competing in local science fairs during that era. Although he was said to be only an average student, he took home multiple prizes over the years, including one for another homemade telescope. He spent much of his spare time reading about astronomy in the local library, and he was particularly fond of visiting Chicago's Adler **Planetarium**, the oldest in the nation.

After graduating from high school in 1957, Carruthers entered the University of Illinois, where he majored in physics and focused on aerospace engineering and astronomy. After earning a bachelor's degree in 1961, Carruthers remained at the school to earn a master's degree in nuclear engineering in 1962 and a doctoral degree in aeronautical engineering in 1964.

While still in high school, Carruthers had read about the US Naval Research Laboratory (NRL), which had been opened in 1923. The idea for the facility has been credited to famed inventor Thomas Edison, who also agreed to head a panel of civilian experts advising the Navy about science and technology. When the NRL started work, researchers did pioneering studies of high-frequency radio and underwater sound **propagation**; the country's first effective radar system was built there.

By 1964, when Carruthers was awarded a National Science Foundation grant to work at the NRL, the facility had expanded its mission to include such wide-ranging projects as monitoring the behavior of the Sun and measuring the dimensions of space. Carruthers was soon hired as a full-time research physicist at the NRL's E. O.

Carruthers did groundbreaking work at this lab in Washington, D.C.

Hurlburt Center for Space Research. There he sought ways in which to create visual images that would help scientists better understand the physical elements of deep space. He

concentrated on UV emissions, which had the potential to provide good clues about the celestial objects that interested researchers. Because the Earth's atmosphere absorbs most UV emissions from space, a UV imaging device that could be placed on the Moon, Carruthers reasoned, would presumably provide a lot of information.

In late 1969 Carruthers received a patent for a type of spectrograph—a device that uses a prism to show the spectrum of light produced by an element or elements—and during a rocket flight the following year, his invention was used to prove the existence of molecular hydrogen in interstellar space—indicating to scientists that plants were not the only source of oxygen for the Earth. The results were even more impressive when the Apollo 16 astronauts set the camera system up on the surface of the Moon. Stars 100 times fainter than were visible to the human eye were recorded, as well as the Large Magellanic Cloud, a satellite galaxy of the Milky Way. Perhaps most importantly, for the first time ever, researchers could measure the level of pollutants in the Earth's upper atmosphere. For his work on the project, which resulted in almost 200 frames of film being obtained, Carruthers was awarded NASA's Exceptional Scientific Achievement Medal.

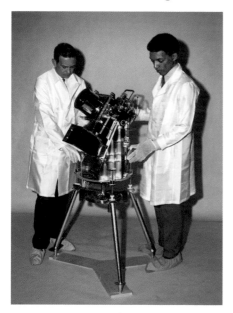

Carruthers (right) examines the spectrograph he helped develop for use in space.

While the system had to be left on the Moon upon Apollo 16's return, another version was used on the 1974 SkyLab, America's first space station. Among other noteworthy accomplishments made possible by Carruthers's work are ultraviolet images of Halley's Comet and an image captured during the Air Force ARGOS mission of a Leonid shower meteor entering the Earth's atmosphere. (The latter marked the first time a meteor image had been obtained in the far ultraviolet by a space-borne camera.)

Carruthers has received numerous laurels for his work, including the 1987 Black Engineer of the Year title; 2003 induction into the National Inventors Hall of Fame; and the 2011 National Medal of Technology and Innovation, one of the highest civilian honors awarded in the U.S.

He is widely recognized for his efforts to educate the next generation of scientists and technologists. He helped create an apprenticeship program that gave high school students the chance to work at the NRL, for example, and he has sponsored numerous science-related programs in Washington, D.C., public schools. Since 2002 he has taught a course on Earth and Space Science at Howard University, one of the nation's most highly regarded historically black institutions of higher learning. ●

Words to Understand

oral history
the collection and study of historical information about individuals, families, and noteworthy events using audio and video recordings or interview transcripts

mission specialist
an astronaut assigned to a specific portion of the mission, for example, medical experiments or technical challenges

Chapter 2

Guy Bluford

"I felt an awesome responsibility, and I took the responsibility very seriously, of being a role model and opening another door to black Americans, but the important thing is not that I am black, but that I did a good job as a scientist and an astronaut," Guy Bluford once said. Few would argue with the fact that Bluford, who in 1983 became the first African-American man ever to travel in space, has succeeded admirably on each one of those counts—as role model, pioneer, scientist, and astronaut.

Guion "Guy" Bluford was born in Philadelphia, Pennsylvania, on November 22, 1942. He has pointed out that unlike many black men of his age, he represents the third generation in his family to attend college. His father was a mechanical engineer, and his mother worked as a special-education

Born:
1942

Nationality:
American

Achievements:
Decorated Air Force pilot who became the first African American in space

teacher. While the Civil Rights Movement was gaining traction during his youth, Bluford, who lived in a row house in one of Philadelphia's predominately black neighborhoods, felt far removed from those struggles.

"I grew up in an environment where I didn't see all of that, and I felt that I could do anything I wanted to do," he said in an **oral history** interview archived at Pennsylvania State University, his alma mater. "I didn't find any problem at all in [aspiring to be] an aerospace engineer."

Bluford was thus somewhat surprised upon graduating from Philadelphia's Overbrook Senior High School in 1960 and entering Penn State, as the school is generally called, to find himself one of very few people of color there. With some 25,000 students enrolled, fewer than 500 were black. The percentage dwindled even more dismally in the engineering programs; Bluford was the only black student studying aerospace engineering for his entire time there.

Feeling isolated because of his race was only one in a multitude of challenges Bluford faced in college. He had led a relatively sheltered life at home and rarely dated, so he found the prospect of being around crowds of single female students both maddeningly distracting and daunting. Additionally, he lacked effective study skills and failed freshman English, a situation that affected his grade point average and caused him to feel that he was digging himself out of an academic hole for several semesters. "People [always] assume that things were easy for me…that I did well in school and was a brain," he said in the oral history. "But

Bluford flew many missions for the Air Force in airplanes like this F-4 during his time in Vietnam.

no. My success was based on other characteristics."

At the time he attended, participation in the Reserve Officers Training Corps (ROTC) was mandatory for all of Penn State's male freshmen and sophomores, so when he graduated in 1964, he had a bachelor's degree in aerospace engineering, a commission in the US Air Force, and a private pilot's license he had earned as part of his advanced ROTC program.

As an Air Force pilot, Bluford flew 144 combat missions during the Vietnam War, many of them directly over North Vietnam, earning numerous military decorations. When he had completed his tours of duty, Bluford enrolled at the Air Force Institute of Technology in Ohio, where he earned a master's degree in aerospace engineering in 1974 and a doctoral degree four years later.

In 1978, the year Bluford earned his Ph.D., NASA was in the process of developing its Space Transportation System (STS), more commonly known as the space shuttle program, and was seeking to recruit a new group of astronauts. They were not only looking for experienced pilots, but also scientists and technologists who would serve as **mission specialists**. Bluford applied and was accepted as a mission specialist. He was one of 35 new astronauts hired that year, among them six women (including Sally Ride, who became the first American woman in space) and two other black men: Fred Gregory and Ron McNair. The three knew that one of them would be chosen as the first African-American astronaut to fly into space, but Bluford remembers feeling no special rivalry. "I didn't push for it, but I was pleasantly surprised by it," he recalled in his oral history interview of being tapped for the honor. "There was a lot of publicity upfront associated with it, and I tried to keep it under control so it didn't get out of hand."

He was only partially successful at keeping

Bluford flew on four different Space Shuttle missions during his time with NASA.

publicity at bay, as hundreds of excited people turned up to watch on August 30, 1983, when the space shuttle *Challenger* took off in the middle of a rainy night from the Kennedy Space Center in Florida with him aboard. *Challenger* orbited the Earth 98 times before landing at Edwards Air Force Base, in California, on the night of September 5, 1983. Over the course of those few days its crew of seven launched a communications satellite for the government of India, made contact with a communications satellite that had gone off-course, conducted multiple scientific experiments, and tested the shuttle's robotic arm. Bluford later flew on three other missions in 1985, 1991, and 1992. By the time Bluford retired, in 1993, he had logged 688 hours in space.

Bluford, who was inducted into the International Space Hall of Fame in 1997, has worked extensively in the private sector since leaving NASA, taking on executive roles in companies such as Northrop Grumman.

He feels not only great pride about having been an astronaut, but also great joy. Listening to audio recordings of his first space flight, Bluford discovered that he had been laughing ecstatically, if unconsciously, all the way into orbit. He once told an audience, "The sad thing about a shuttle mission is when you hit the point in your checklist where it says 'bring vehicle home.'" ●

Guy Bluford:
First African-American in space

Words to Understand

cosmonaut
an astronaut in the space program of Russia or the former Soviet Union

pessimistic
not sure or unconvinced of the possible success of something

tenure
a specific period of time one holds an office or a job

Chapter 3

Charles Bolden

Born:
1946

Nationality:
American

Achievements:
**Scientist and astronaut
who has become the
director of NASA**

Since 2009 Charles Frank Bolden, Jr., a former astronaut, has served as the head of NASA. "It's a long way from the segregated south to low Earth orbit, but I am fortunate to have made the journey," wrote Bolden in an essay posted on the official White House website to celebrate Black History Month. He is the first African-American ever to oversee the nation's space program.

Bolden was born on August 19, 1946, in Columbia, South Carolina, into a family that greatly valued education and community involvement. His father, Charles, Sr., who had served in the US Army during World War II, was a high school teacher and football coach. A local stadium was later named for Charles Bolden Sr. Bolden's mother, Ethel, began her career as a teacher and ultimately became a librarian; she established the first elementa-

ry-school library at a black school in Columbia's then-segregated education system. In 1968, during the turbulent years of the Civil Rights movement, she was among the first African-American professionals to work in the area's predominately white high schools. "My parents were probably the biggest influences on my life," Bolden wrote. "Not only growing up, but still, today."

Bolden attended local public schools and was a frequent patron of the public library. (It is customary for astronauts to take meaningful personal artifacts into space with them, and Bolden once took his childhood library card, which was then put on display at that Charleston library.) Thanks to his parents' emphasis on education, he attended many science camps and summer programs.

After Bolden graduated from C. A. Johnson High School in 1964, he sought to gain entry into the US Naval Academy in Annapolis, Maryland. It was, as he has recalled, "an uphill battle." Prospective cadets were required to obtain an endorsement from a congressman, and no one in the South Carolina delegation would speak up on behalf of an African-American candidate. Finally, after a determined Bolden wrote a letter to President Lyndon B. Johnson explaining his plight, William Dawson of Illinois, a veteran of World War I and the only serving black member of Congress (during some portions of his **tenure**), stepped up to provide the needed nomination.

In 1968 Bolden earned a bachelor's degree in electrical science from the Academy and was commissioned as a second lieutenant in the US Marine Corps. He became a pilot, and in the early 1970s, during the Vietnam War, he flew more than 100 combat missions.

In 1977 Bolden earned a master's degree in systems management from the University of Southern California. He went next to Maryland, where attended the US Naval Test Pilot

Bolden is pictured on the flight deck of his first shuttle mission in 1986.

School, a highly competitive program for experienced military pilots and officers. Graduating in 1979, he participated in multiple test projects involving A-6 and A-7 attack aircraft.

Bolden was friendly with fellow South Carolina native Ronald McNair, who had been accepted for NASA astronaut training in 1978. McNair, who would later perish in the space shuttle *Challenger* tragedy, was a tireless champion for other blacks who wanted to explore space. In 1980 he convinced a **pessimistic** Bolden to at least try to gain admittance into the highly selective program. Somewhat to his surprise, Bolden was accepted. During his time as an American astronaut, he made four spaceflights: a 1986 mission on the shuttle *Columbia* to launch a communications satellite; a 1990 shuttle *Discovery* mission to deploy the Hubble Space Telescope; a 1992 flight on the shuttle *Atlantis*, which was carrying the Atmospheric Laboratory for Applications

and Science; and a 1994 flight that marked the first time a NASA mission had included a Russian cosmonaut. (Bolden was commander of those last two missions.)

Bolden retired from NASA in 1994 and returned to the Marine Corps., taking part in a number of important military operations and earning several promotions (along with such laurels as the Defense Superior Service Medal and the Distinguished Flying Cross). He served as Deputy Commanding General of the 1st Marine Expeditionary Force in the Pacific in 1997, for example, and the following year he was named Commanding General of the 1st Marine Expeditionary Force Forward in support of Operation Desert Thunder in Kuwait. Then, after being promoted to Major General in 1998, he was named Deputy Commander of US Forces in Japan.

Bolden retired from the Marine Corps in 2003 and entered private industry. He returned to public service in 2009, however, when President Barack Obama tapped him to head NASA. "When I was a young man, my service as NASA's first African

Bolden spoke at the 2011 event at which the final Space Shuttle mission landed.

American Administrator under the Nation's first Black President would have been nearly unthinkable," wrote Bolden, who was inducted into the US Astronaut Hall of Fame in 2006.

Bolden is frequently called upon to be the public face of the space agency, and he has proven to be a patient, engaging, and even humorous spokesperson, particularly with young audiences. Speaking to a group of British schoolchildren in 2015, he was asked how soon it would be before humans could land on Mars, he replied that it was contingent upon inventing "a toilet that's not going to break on the way there." ●

Words to Understand

residency
a period of advanced medical training and education that consists of supervised practice of a specialty

space adaptation syndrome
commonly known as "space sickness," the condition can cause vertigo, nausea, headaches, and vomiting

Chapter 4

Bernard A. Harris

Born:
1956

Nationality:
American

Achievements:
Medical doctor who became astronaut and made first spacewalk by an African American

While Guy Bluford (see profile on page 18) was the first black man in space, Bernard Anthony Harris, Jr., had a similarly noteworthy honor: in 1995 he became the first African-American astronaut ever to perform an extra-vehicular activity (EVA), more commonly known as a spacewalk.

"I remember feeling [very] small [because we were] just a speck on the horizon," Harris recalled during a speech he gave at the Worcester Polytechnic Institute in 2015. "But [later] I went from being this small person to being larger than life, with the realization that I was doing something very few people had done before. That I was one of about 350 people who've ever gone in space, that I was one of about 70 people that had ever done a spacewalk. And that I was about 1 in 15 of us who were African American."

Harris was born on June 26, 1956, in Temple, Texas. Until he was six years old his family, which included an older sister and younger brother, lived in Houston. That year, however, his parents, Bernard Sr., and Gussie, divorced, and Gussie took the three children to live with her mother in the tiny town of Oakwood. A teacher by training, Gussie worked as a truck-stop cook until one day discovering that the Bureau of Indian Affairs was seeking applicants to teach at reservation schools. Upon being hired, she moved to a Navajo reservation in Greasewood, Arizona, by herself, but within a few months she had settled in, earned enough money to buy a car, and picked up Harris and his siblings for the trip to their new home.

While theirs was a small, cramped house, it struck Harris as a marked improvement over their quarters in Oakwood, and Arizona was a revelation to him. He recalled in his speech, "[My mother] took us to a land of grand canyons and painted deserts where…I could be free, where I could discover what my dreams and what my ambitions are."

Life improved further when Harris was eleven and Gussie remarried. He grew close to his new stepfather, a policeman, and often cites him as an early role model.

When Harris was thirteen the family moved to San Antonio, Texas, and he discovered role models of a different sort. That year, Neil Armstrong took man's first steps on the Moon, and Harris was riveted. He joined science and rocket clubs and became an avid fan of science fiction books and television shows, particularly *Star Trek*. He was far from a "geek," however. He played football, basketball, and soccer, and he formed his own R&B band, which played local venues on the weekends. When not studying, playing sports, or making music, Harris worked as a grocery store bagger, hotel janitor, and landscaper to earn money.

With his ambition to become an astronaut firmly set at the age of thirteen, Harris, who graduated from Sam Houston High School in 1974, investigated colleges and learned that there was no one definite path to that goal. He discovered, however, that there were physicians involved in the space program, and he set his sights on medical school. After earning a bachelor's degree in biology from the University of Houston in 1978, he entered the Texas Tech University School of Medicine. Upon signing up for a **residency** in internal medicine at the renowned Mayo Clin-

Harris studied here at Texas Tech University's med school.

ic, he was gratified to find that one of his supervisors had worked for NASA in the past.

Harris knew that his chances of being accepted into the space program would be better if he had experience as a researcher, and upon completing his residency, he accepted a fellowship at the Ames Research Center, a world-class facility in California, affiliated with NASA.

In 1987, after the fellowship was completed, Harris applied for the astronaut program. That year 15 people were accepted, and Harris was devastated not to make the final cut. He was, however, offered a job as a clinical scientist and flight surgeon at the Johnson Space Center. He consoled himself with the thought that he could prove himself in that capacity and try again.

His instincts were correct; after working diligently at Ames to research **Space Adaptation Syndrome** and other areas, he applied for a second time and in 1991 was chosen for astronaut training.

In 1993, Harris took part in his first mission, flying on the space shuttle *Columbia*. With him he took a flag blessed by a Navajo medicine man, marking the first time a Navajo artifact had been sent into space. In 1995, he was part of the crew of the *Discovery*, which had been sent to rendezvous with the Russian space station Mir. On that mission Harris, donning a suit that weighed 350 pounds, became the first African American to walk in space.

During his time as a mission specialist with NASA, Harris completed almost 150 experiments onboard the shuttles, logged well over 400 hours in space, and traveled some 7 million miles. After retiring in 1996, he embarked on a career in private industry with such high-tech companies as SPACEHAB and Vesalius Ventures.

In 1998, the former astronaut—whose many honors include a NASA Space Flight Medal, a NASA Award of Merit, and a Horatio Alger Award—launched the Harris Foundation, a Houston-based organization whose mission is "to invest in community-based initiatives to support education, health and wealth [and] support programs that empower individuals, in particular minorities and other economically and/or socially disadvantaged, to recognize their potential and pursue their dreams." ●

Harris now works to encourage young people to follow science careers.

Bernard Harris:
Astronaut, doctor, leader

Words to Understand

hepatitis
a disease that involves inflammation of the liver

Ivy League
a group of eight universities in the Northeastern United States that are widely regarded to be the best colleges in the country

Chapter 5

Mae C. Jemison

Born:
1956

Nationality:
American

Achievements:
**Medical doctor who became
first African–American
woman in space**

At a 2009 research conference for minority students, Mae Jemison told her young audience, "Never be limited by other people's limited imaginations....If you adopt their attitudes, then the possibility won't exist because you'll have already shut it out." It was advice that Jemison, the first black woman in space, had heeded her entire life.

Mae Carol Jemison was born on October 17, 1956, in Decatur, Alabama. Her father, Charlie, worked as a roofer, maintenance engineer, and taxi driver, and her mother, Dorothy, returned to school as an adult to become an elementary school teacher. They relocated the family to Chicago when Jemison was just three years old, because of the better school system there, and Jemison often refers to Chicago as her hometown. The move served its purpose admirably, and all

three of the children excelled; Jemison's older sister, Ada, became a child psychiatrist, and her older brother, Charles, became a successful real estate consultant.

Jemison was a bright child who learned to read well before she started kindergarten, and by the age of five she was telling people she intended to become a scientist; she devoured Madeline L'Engle's *A Wrinkle in Time* trilogy because the books featured female scientists and heroines. Her parents were deeply supportive of her goals; once, when a minor wound became infected, she set up an experiment using her own pus, and they let her complete it rather than insisting that it be thrown away. While that tale might make Jemison seem like an unpopular outcast, she was, to the contrary, an active, social figure during her school years. She participated in student government, appeared in school plays, and seriously studied dance, which she credits with giving her an appreciation for hard work and physical strength.

During her time in the Peace Corps, Jemison worked with children like these in Kenya.

Jemison came of age during the Civil Rights Movement, and once, when she was twelve, the mayor of Chicago called in the National Guard to quell demonstrations in that city. When the heavily armed Guardsmen marched through her predominately black neighborhood, she was frightened and angry. Later in life, she would remember that day and remind herself that she enjoyed the same rights as an American as those intimidating National Guard members.

When she graduated with honors from Chicago's Morgan Park High School in 1973, Jemison won a National Achievement Scholarship to attend Stanford University in California, where she served as the head of the Black Student Union, acted in student plays, and learned to speak Russian and Swahili. In 1977, she earned a Bachelor of Science degree in chemical engineering, while also fulfilling the requirements for a Bachelor of Arts degree in African and Afro-American studies. She subsequently entered Cornell University Medical College, and while earning her M.D. degree, she studied in Cuba and Kenya and did volunteer work at a refugee camp in Thailand.

Jemison earned her medical degree in 1981 and worked briefly as a general practitioner. From 1983 to 1985, she was a member of the Peace Corps, serving as a medical officer in West Africa. Following that adventure, which found her providing medical care, supervising pharmacies, conducting research on **hepatitis**, and more, Jemison became determined to pursue yet another goal: becoming an astronaut.

In October 1985, she applied to the astronaut training program, but the *Challenger* disaster in January 1986 disrupted NASA's selection process. When Jemison reap-

plied the following year, however, she became one of 15 candidates chosen from more than 2,000 hopefuls; she was the first black woman ever admitted into the training program, and when the shuttle *Endeavour* launched on September 12, 1992, with her aboard as a mission specialist, she became the first black woman to orbit the Earth. "I felt like I belonged right there in space," she told one interviewer. "I realized I would feel comfortable anywhere in the universe—because I belonged to and was a part of it, as much as any star, planet, asteroid, comet, or nebula."

During the *Endeavour*'s eight-day flight—a cooperative mission between the U.S. and Japan—Jemison helped conduct experiments on weightlessness and motion sickness, and she was a co-investigator on a major bone cell research project flown on the mission. When the *Endeavour* touched down at the Kennedy Space Center on September 20, Jemison had logged 190 hours, 30 minutes, and 23 seconds in space.

After leaving NASA in early 1993, Jemison accepted a post as a professor of Environmental Studies at Dartmouth College, an **Ivy League** institution in New Hampshire, where she directed the school's Jemison Institute for Advancing Technology in Developing Countries. (She is now an adjunct professor of Community and Family Medicine there.) She also founded the Jemison Group, a technology company that helps design power systems for developing countries and satellite-based telecommunications systems aimed at facilitating health care in remote areas. She launched a second company, BioSentient, a few years later, in order to develop mobile equipment that monitors a patient's vital signs.

In addition to her business ventures, in 1994 Jemison launched the Dorothy Jemison Foundation for Excellence, named after her mother, and under its auspices she has long run The Earth We Share (TEWS), an annual four-week science camp for students aged 12 to 16.

Jemison often speaks to school groups about her experiences as an astronaut.

Among her many honors are a Black Achievement Trailblazers Award, a Kilby Science Award, induction into the National Medical Association Hall of Fame, and numerous honorary doctorates. She has appeared on many television shows celebrating science and black history, and she was once even featured in an episode of *Star Trek: The Next Generation*, playing a character named Lieutenant Palmer. ●

Mae Jemison: First African-American woman in space

Words to Understand

astrophysicist
a scientist who studies the physical and chemical properties and structures of stars, planets, and other objects in outer space

Kuiper Belt
a disc-shaped region of icy objects beyond the orbit of Neptune, with Pluto being its best-known feature

Chapter 6

Neil deGrasse Tyson

Most **astrophysicists** are not well-known enough to get hate mail from the general public, but thanks to his many television appearances, social media posts, magazine columns, and books, Neil deGrasse Tyson is. When Tyson, the director of New York City's Hayden Planetarium, decreed that Pluto would no longer be referred to as the ninth planet in exhibits at the popular venue, letters poured in, many of them from children, who decried his characterization of their favorite celestial body as a mere object in the **Kuiper Belt**. He fanned those flames in early 2015, after NASA reached Pluto for the first time, tweeting to his almost 4 million Twitter followers: "Dear Pluto, lookin' good. But you're still [only] a Dwarf Planet—get over it. Love, Neil deGrasse Tyson."

Born:
1958

Nationality:
American

Achievements:
Astrophysicist and director of leading planetarium; TV host and frequent spokesman for science in the public interest

Tyson's ability to relate to the public in a humorous way and to explain complex astrophysical concepts to laypeople is much of the reason for his fame. He has worked hard to be considered simply a brilliant scientist, rather than pigeonholed as a brilliant black scientist.

"I no longer do Black History Month talks," he told an interviewer for *Black Enterprise* magazine in 2011. "If that's when you think of inviting me to talk, then clearly if I never show up in your thoughts the other 11 months I'm not as visible a scientist as I should be."

While he is happy to advise any young person considering a career in science, he cautioned the interviewer, "I think the concept of role model is overrated. If I required a black person who became a scientist who grew up in the Bronx to have come before me, I would have never become what I am."

Tyson was born on October 5, 1958, in New York City. He was given his middle name in honor of his paternal grandmother, Altima de Grasse, who hailed from the British West Indies. Tyson's family lived in the New York City borough of the Bronx, first in an area called Castle Hill and then in the predominately white and affluent neighborhood of Riverdale. Theirs was a household that highly valued education. His parents, Cyril and Sunchita, took their children to museums and cultural events as often as possible, and at dinnertime, Tyson and his two siblings were often called upon to make formal presentations about their day. (All three became great successes; Tyson's older brother, Stephen, is a Fulbright award-winning artist and professor, while his younger sister, Lynn, works in the financial sector.)

Tyson, who attended public elementary and middle schools, became deeply interested in space after attending a program at the American Museum of Natural History's Hayden Planetarium. Shortly after that visit, he was on a family trip in rural Pennsylvania, and for the first time he saw the night sky unobstructed by city lights. "What is an embarrassingly urban thought:

The Hayden Planetarium in New York City

I look up at the night sky from the finest mountaintops in the world and I would say, 'It reminds me of the Hayden Planetarium,'" Tyson has admitted to interviewers. "But so strong was that imprint that I'm certain that I had no choice in the matter, that in fact the universe called me."

While attending the Bronx High School of Science, Tyson competed on the wrestling team and served as editor-in-chief of the *Physical Science Journal*. He also attended astronomy courses that were given by the Hayden Planetarium, and he considers that period one of the most important

and formative of his life. Tyson became so well known in the astronomy community for his intelligence and passion that famed cosmologist Carl Sagan, then a faculty member at Cornell University, tried to recruit him.

While he greatly admired Sagan, Tyson chose instead to study at Harvard University, where he earned a bachelor's degree in physics in 1980. In 1983, Tyson received a master's degree in astronomy from the University of Texas at Austin, and he followed that with master's and doctoral degrees in astrophysics from Columbia University, in 1989 and 1991, respectively.

In 1994, he joined the Hayden Planetarium, which had played such a big part in his life, as a staff scientist. In 1996, he became its director. He told reporters, "When I was a kid, there were scientists and educators on the staff at the Hayden Planetarium who invested their time and energy in my enlightenment, and I've never forgotten that. And to end up back there as its director, I feel this deep sense of duty…that I serve in the same capacity for people who come through the facility today."

For a group selfie, Tyson (right) is joined by fellow science educator Bill Nye and President Obama.

As director, Tyson oversaw a $200-million reconstruction of the planetarium, which was completed in 2000. Part of the American Museum of Natural History's Rose Center for Earth and Space, the planetarium is housed in an 87-foot sphere, which appears to float within a six-story glass cube.

Tyson is busy in all media. For years, he appeared regularly as a host on the PBS series, *Nova*, for example, and in 2014 he starred in *Cosmos: A Spacetime Odyssey*, a documentary miniseries. Most recently, he began hosting the National Geographic Channel's *StarTalk*, discussing science and culture with a variety of guests.

Among Tyson's many awards is the Public Welfare Medal from the National Academy of Sciences for his "extraordinary role in exciting the public about the wonders of science." His television appearances, magazine columns, radio shows, and many layperson-friendly books are all aimed at that goal. "[You must be capable of] analysis of the information that comes your way," he has said. "And that's what I don't see enough of in this world. There's a level of gullibility that leaves people susceptible to being taken advantage of. I see science literacy as kind of a vaccine against charlatans who would try to exploit your ignorance." ●

Neil deGrasse Tyson: Spreading the word on science

Words to Understand

anisotropy
the state of having properties that differ when measured in different directions

altimeter
an instrument for measuring altitude

topographic
relating to, or showing topography (the shape, height, and depth of the features of a place)

Chapter 7

Aprille Ericcson

Born:
1963

Nationality:
American

Achievements:
Engineer and space scientist who has done important work on many NASA projects and missions

For decades, Aprille Ericcson has been one of NASA's most well-known aerospace engineers and is often included on lists of the most powerful women working in technology. She never forgets how hard it was to reach that pinnacle and the help she received along the way. Invoking her favorite quote, she has said, "If you see a turtle sitting on top of a fence post, you know he had help getting there....My greatest challenge [now] is climbing the ladder of success and pulling others behind me."

Ericcson, the oldest of four daughters, was born in the New York City borough of Brooklyn, on April 1, 1963. Her parents, Corrine and Henry, separated when she was eight. Ericcson grew up in a hardscrabble neighborhood called Bedford-Stuyvesant and lived in a crime-ridden housing project

on DeKalb Avenue. An enthusiastic Girl Scout, she went camping each summer, which provided her with a change of scene from her harsh, urban environs.

During a time when schools were integrating, she was bussed to P.S. 199, in another section of Brooklyn, and she went on to attend Marine Park Junior High School, where she was the only black student in the gifted and talented program. In addition to her academic prowess, she participated in the school band and played on the girls' basketball team. During her final year of junior high, she won second place in a major science fair and scored in the 90s on all her citywide exams. Although she excelled at science and math, she did not focus immediately on careers related to those topics, dreaming at various times of being an artist, lawyer, or pro athlete.

New York City has three elite and rigorous public high schools—the Bronx School of Science, Stuyvesant, and Brooklyn Technical—and Ericcson passed the highly competitive entrance exam for all three. She chose instead to accept a full scholarship to the Cambridge School of Weston, in Massachusetts, where students are offered more than 300 courses and encouraged to pursue a variety of interests. While the school had boarding facilities, Ericcson lived with her grandparents and attended as a day student.

As in junior high, Ericcson was a well-rounded student, excelling at academics while playing basketball and softball and volunteering to work with local children. During the summer following her third year at the Cambridge School,

At the Massachusetts Institute of Technology in Cambridge, Mass., Ericcson studied advanced physics and engineering.

she took part in a program at the Massachusetts Institute of Technology (MIT), and her ambitions crystallized. She decided then to pursue a career in science and technology.

Upon graduating from high school, Ericcson entered MIT to major in Aeronautical and Astronautical Engineering. Thanks to the school's focus on hands-on research, even for undergraduates, she participated in several exciting projects, including developing a fiber optic laser gyroscope at MIT's Applied Physics Laboratory and working in the Space Systems Laboratory to create a computer database of buoyancy measurements generated by NASA.

Ericcson's goals became even clearer thanks to her work on those projects, and she began dreaming of participating in manned space missions. However, in 1986, the year she earned her bachelor's degree from MIT, the *Challenger* disaster put the future of the shuttle program in jeopardy, and Ericcson's application was placed on hold.

Thus, instead of heading into the astronaut-training program, Ericcson headed to Howard University, a well-regarded historically black institution. She majored in mechanical engineering with a specialization in aerospace engineering, and earned her master's degree in 1992. Thanks to a cooperative program with NASA, Ericcson was able to join NASA that year as an engineer, while still doing coursework towards her doctoral degree. She was assigned to the Goddard Space Flight Center (GSFC) in Maryland, where she worked on guidance, navigation, and control systems.

In 1995, when Ericcson graduated from Howard with a Ph.D. in Mechanical Engineering, she became the first black, female student in the history of the school to do so. She was also the first black, female employee at GSFC to earn a doctoral degree. Since then, she has worked her way up the ranks at NASA and has held such posts as Instrument Program Manager and Manager of the Applied Engineering and Technology Directorate. She currently coordinates all Goddard small business partnership activities and technology infusion initiatives.

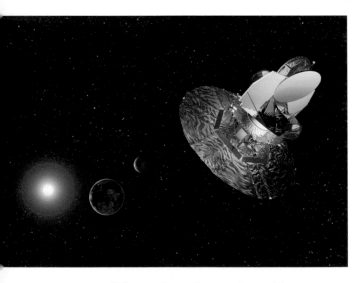

Ericcson's probes and machines are sent into space on satellites to beam back important data.

Among the NASA projects for which Ericcson has been most celebrated are the Microwave **Anisotropy** Probe, which provided the first detailed full-sky map of the microwave background radiation in the universe; a satellite that uses laser technology to calculate how the polar ice cap surface is changing; LOLA, a lunar orbiter laser **altimeter**, which created a **topographic** map of the Moon's landscape; and the instruments used in the attempt to bring dust from the lower atmosphere of Mars back to Earth.

Ericcson has been an adjunct professor at Howard, teaching undergraduate courses in Automatic Control Theory, Advanced Dynamics, and Vibrations Analysis, and she has also sat on the university's board of trustees. Long known for her efforts to interest women and minorities in math, science, and engineering, she speaks in numerous elementary, middle, and high school classrooms each year, stressing the importance of those topics and using her personal story to inspire others. ●

Aprille Ericcson:
Space engineer and inventor

Whether you're interested in inventing a device that will further our understanding of space like George Carruthers, or educating the public about the cosmos like Neil deGrasse Tyson, it's important to take as many high-level math and science courses as possible while you're still in high school. Many of the people profiled in this volume studied engineering—particularly aeronautical engineering—and that requires entering college with a firm grasp of subjects like physics and calculus. (And even if you choose a non-engineering path, like physicians Mae Jemison and Bernard Harris, science and math are vital.)

Settling upon a college is never an easy task, but several websites and publications like *U.S. News & World Re-*

Space Camp!

Space Camp, located at the US Space & Rocket Center, in Huntsville, Alabama, allows attendees of all ages to take part in simulated missions, walk in a low-gravity environment, and take a spin in the device once used to test astronauts' susceptibility to motion sickness.

Their Advanced Space Academy, aimed at teens, is a college-accredited program that provides one hour of freshman-level general science credit—and the chance to try out the Underwater Astronaut Trainer, study orbital mechanics, and design a spacesuit.

Financial aid is available for qualified candidates, and more information can be found at http://www.spacecamp.com/.

Space engineers start with experiments; these men are working on a new drag chute that might be used to land a probe.

port maintain lists of the best schools in the U.S., and those are good places to start your search. Would you prefer a large school or small? Is a prestigious, recognizable name important to you? Would you be most comfortable at one of the fine historically black colleges and universities (HBCUs) in the country? With a bit of research, you can find an institution that meets all of your requirements.

If choosing a college is hard, figuring out how to pay for it can be even harder. Fortunately, there are many sources of financial aid and scholarships, and as schools increasingly focus on attracting greater numbers of minority students to Science, Technology, Engineering, and Math (STEM) fields, the possibilities are expanding. Groups like the National Society of Black Engineers (NSBE) and the National Action Council for Minorities in Engineering (NACME), and the

National Organization for the Professional Advancement of Black Chemists and Chemical Engineers (NOBCChE) are good sources of information, and alphabetized lists of every scholarship available (even very obscure ones) abound on the Internet. Again, research is key!

Where you ultimately decide to go to school is just one factor in your future success, however. Internships and volunteer positions can be a great way to learn more about your chosen field, and NASA has sever-

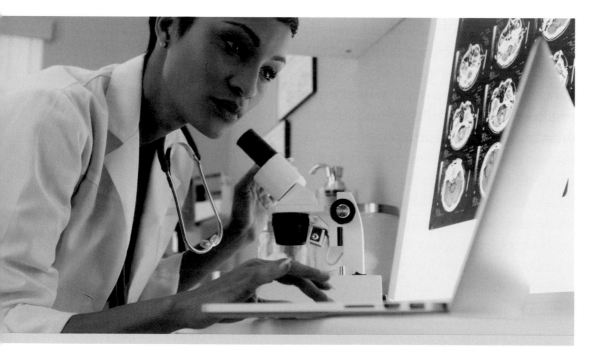

Working in space science can be part of many science careers, such as studying the effects of space travel on the human body.

al student programs in place that can help you stand out when it's time to apply for a job, including Pathways (http://nasajobs.nasa.gov/studentopps/employment/iep.htm), which provides students enrolled in a variety of educational institutions with paid opportunities to work in agencies and explore possible careers while still in school.

Suppose you've done all the research and decided that no other space-related job besides astronaut will do? Be prepared for hard work and a LOT of competition! NASA requires that in addition to meeting the physical conditions, all astronaut candidates have a bachelor's degree from an accredited institution in engineering, biological science, physical science, or mathematics, followed by either an advanced degree, at least three years of related, progressively responsible, professional experience, or 1,000 hours commanding a jet aircraft. ●

Text-Dependent Questions

1. What is the name of the oldest planetarium in the U.S. and where is it located?

2. How fast did space shuttles travel?

3. How much does the suit worn by astronauts during space-walks weigh?

4. How long was Mae Jemison in orbit?

5. What planetarium does Neil deGrasse Tyson direct?

6. What did Aprille Ericcson develop as a student in MIT's Applied Physics Laboratory?

Suggested Research Projects

1. Many websites give directions for making home-made spectroscopes with cardboard tubing. What do you think would happen if you looked at various light sources through a spectroscope?

2. The space shuttle program lasted for three decades and 135 missions. Make a timeline of noteworthy shuttle missions.

3. The Space Foundation is a nonprofit organization. Investigate its mission and activities.

4. Astronauts go on spacewalks to do several important jobs. Research some of them and write a paragraph about what it would be like to perform those tasks in space.

5. Watch an episode of one of Neil deGrasse Tyson's television shows. Make a list of the times he uses humor to explain a scientific concept or make a point.

6. Aprille Ericcson turned to mechanical engineering to obtain a job at NASA when she was not admitted into the astronaut-training program. What other jobs does the agency have for non-astronauts? Research the educational requirements and work duties of those positions.

Find Out More

Websites

www.nasa.gov

NASA's official site contains fascinating information on the agency's history, numerous photos, live updates from the International Space Station, career advice, and much more.

BlackStudents.com

This is a comprehensive online guide to scholarships, financial aid and more for African-American students of all interests, including aeronautics.

Books

David, Leonard and Scott Sacknoff. *Space Careers*. Bethesda, MD: International Space Business Council, 2015.
This guide includes a foreword by famed astronaut Buzz Aldrin as well as valuable advice about colleges, scholarships, and job opportunities.

Hardesty, Von. *Black Wings: Courageous Stories of African Americans in Aviation and Space History*. Washington D.C.: Smithsonian Institute Press, 2008.
A book that focuses on the many contributions of black aviators, pilots, and astronauts.

Paul, Richard and Steven Moss. *We Could Not Fail: The First African Americans in the Space Program*. Austin: University of Texas Press, 2015.
This books examines the start of the Space Age against the backdrop of the Civil Rights Movement and says that Presidents John F. Kennedy and Lyndon Johnson skillfully used the space program as an agent for social change by encouraging NASA to hire numerous African Americans in key roles.

Series Glossary of Key Terms

botany the study of plant biology

electron a negatively charged particle in an atom

genome all the DNA in an organism, including all the genes

nanometer a measurement of length that is one-billionth of a meter

nanotechnology manipulation of matter on an atomic or molecular scale

patent a set of exclusive rights granted to an inventor for a limited period of time in exchange for detailed public disclosure of an invention

periodic table the arrangement of all the known elements into a table based on increasing atomic number

protein large molecules in the body responsible for the structure and function of all the tissues in an organism

quantum mechanics the scientific principles that describe how matter on a small scale (such as atoms and electrons) behaves

segregated separated, in this case by race

ultraviolet a type of light, usually invisible, that can cause damage to the skin

Index

Photo credits

About the Author

Mari Rich was educated at Lehman College, part of the public City University of New York. As a writer and editor, she has had many years of experience in the fields of university communications and reference publishing, most notably with the highly regarded periodical *Current Biography*, aimed at high school and college readers. She also edited and wrote for *World Authors, Leaders of the Information Age*, and *Nobel Laureates*. Currently, she spends much of her time writing about engineers and engineering.